Colin Discovers Confidence

I0569173

Creator and illustrator: Patrick Arguin

English translation: Bleu Dactylo

French version written by: Michèle Rappe
Support, coaching and collaboration: Hélène Beaudette

I want to offer my deepest gratitude to Hélène Beaudette.
Her unconditional support and presence allowed TOOLS OF THE HEART to grow and come into form.

A storm is raging!
The wind shakes the oaks of the garden furiously.
Suddenly, an acorn is pulled loose and carried far, far away
from its home.

On its course, the acorn hits a rock and cracks open.
The seed inside falls onto the ground. Luckily, Mother Earth
welcomes it and covers it with all her love.

The little seed is happy. Mother Earth nourishes it, while Father Sun keeps it warm and cozy.

«My name will be Colin!» decides the little seed.

Father Sun and Mother Earth guide Colin in his growth and surround him with their presence and their love.

«The more I grow, the further I feel from Mother Earth!» notices Colin.
«Growing up can sometimes be scary!» he worries.

Colin is worried and cannot sleep.
He wonders what will happen when he becomes a bigger oak.

«What will happen to me?»
he asks the Moon, bright in the sky.

The Moon heard Colin and tells him:
«Inside your heart, there is wisdom,
which can help and guide you.»

«Wisdom!?» worries Colin,
«I have never seen any wisdom.»

«I will tell you how to find it,»
kindly answers the Moon.

Colin closes his eyes and carefully
listens to the Moon.
«Focus on the love inside your heart,»
she says, «and slowly breathe in.»

Colin relaxes.
He feels the calm settling inside him,
and Yellow the elf appears before him.

«You see Colin,» explains the elf, «there is a lot of love and strength inside your heart, and it flows everywhere inside of you, just like your sap.»

Colin feels a sense of well-being and is filled with a beautiful yellow light growing inside of him.

«Now,» says the elf, «focus on the tips of your roots. They are firmly planted in the ground and in touch with the love of Mother Earth.»

Colin can feel his roots and all the strength flowing inside of him.

«You can feel this strength every time you need it,» says Yellow. «It will give you the confidence you need to grow up.»

Colin has grown and is now a strong young oak.
He visits his heart often to meet with Yellow and
to find his sense of well-being and self-confidence.

One morning, terrified birds are flying above Colin.
«A terrible storm is coming from the north of the garden!»
they chirp as they flee the storm.

Colin shivers, he sees the storm approaching, and he can
feel the fear rising within him.

Then he closes his eyes, focuses on his heart to gather all of his strength and confidence.

«My roots are solid,» he thinks, «and I won't fly away!»

When the storm arrives, Colin fearlessly stands it. The strong winds make him sway, but his roots are firmly planted.

He is really proud of himself.

Time has passed. In the garden, there is an oak swaying in the wind. He is not afraid of the furious winds or the storm. It is Colin stretching his branches towards Father Sun and his roots towards Mother Earth.

Remember...

Is it normal to worry sometimes?

Of course! It even happens to grown-ups you know! But the more your confidence grows inside you, the less space there is for fears and worries.

How can I make my confidence grow?

Inside of you, there is a lot of strength and courage but sometimes, you either forget about it, or you think it is gone. By remembering it is there, you can make your confidence grow again. It helps you become strong and confident, just like an oak who relies on its roots during a big storm.

Can I grow roots like a tree?

Absolutely! Close your eyes, breathe in slowly and from your belly, imagine roots growing deep into the Earth. Imagine the force rising inside you, from the bottom of your feet to the top of your head. You can grow roots anytime you need them!

The Book Collection

Tools of the Heart
Fostering Confidence and Self-esteem

1 Father Sun and Mother Earth Create Life
Breathing/Finding your rhythm

Breathing is essential to life; conscious breathing is a simple, yet effective way to regain your calm and well-being by finding your body's rhythm.

2 Fluffy and the Rainbow in his Heart
Meditation/Finding your inner calm

Each one of us has a peaceful place inside their heart. Meditation is a tool that allows you to find your personal space or to go back to it.

3 Colin Discovers Confidence
Grounding/Strengthening your self-confidence

Growing up often comes with its share of fears and hesitations. Growing solid roots helps to build and nurture a positive self-confidence.

4 Colin and Fluffy Become Friends
Knowing yourself/Loving and appreciating

Positive self-confidence and self-esteem are the building blocks of healthy relationships; therefore, learning to appreciate who we are is a treasure for life.

5 The Choice
Insight/Listening to your intuition

Learning to listen to your inner voice and how to trust it, is learning to stay true to yourself in all situations.

6 Colin's Courage
Expressing/Confidence in yourself

Standing up for yourself is not wrong. It is about relying on your self-worth with confidence, to respectfully say what you need to say.

7 Enough is Enough
Self-respect/Daring to be yourself

Developing good communication skills also implies expressing your feelings and needs in a respectful manner, which can sometimes be a challenge!

8 Fluffy Finds his Well-being
Self-awareness/Taking responsibility

Growing up is also about becoming more aware of your emotions and learning to manage them responsibly.

The Meditation Collection

Tools of the Heart

Fostering Confidence and Self-esteem

Specially designed for young children, the guided meditations explore and develop the same themes, as seen in the **Tools of the Heart** book collection. These intend to reinforce the children's knowledge of themselves through their inner space of wisdom, where things can be seen, heard, and felt.

Meditation is also a wonderful tool that children can easily learn to help them self-regulate physically, mentally, and emotionally.

To learn more, go to our website:

www.toolsoftheheart.com

3

www.ingramcontent.com/pod-product-compliance
Lightning Source LLC
Chambersburg PA
CBHW040246150626
46547CB00042B/3251